YOUR
HEALING
IS
KILLING
ME

Your Healing is Killing Me
© 2017 Virginia Grise

Published by Plays Inverse Press
Pittsburgh, PA
www.playsinverse.com

ISBN 13: 978-0-9914183-9-8

First Printing: October 2017
Cover & Illustrations by Zeke Peña
Page design by Tyler Crumrine
Printed in the U.S.A.

**PLAYS
INVERSE**

YOUR HEALING IS KILLING ME

VIRGINIA GRISE

PLAYS INVERSE PRESS
PITTSBURGH, PA
2017

Your Healing is Killing Me was first presented as a performance lecture in 2015 for the Creating New Medical and Health Humanities Programming at the University of California Riverside (funded by the National Endowment for the Humanities), a program where medical school and humanities faculty collaborate to develop medical narratives curricula to improve doctor-patient communication. Invited by Dr. Tiffany López.

Your Healing is Killing Me then received a workshop production at Multicultural Education and Counseling through the Arts (MECA) in Houston, Texas, March 4-5, 2016, as part of a National Performance Network Artist Residency. Directed by Emily Mendelsohn. Invited by Estevan Azcona, performance and residency director.

An excerpt from *Your Healing is Killing Me* was read at the HOT! Festival Little Theater at Dixon Place in New York City, on July 11, 2016. Curated by Casey Llewellyn.

The book manuscript was further developed with Emily Mendelsohn at a residency at Ritual and Research, August 26-September 2, 2016, in Worthington, MA. Invited by David Hurwith.

A reading of *Your Healing is Killing Me*, with Cynthia Bastidas, Dana Chavez, and Lindsay Rico occurred

April 8, 2017 at the New Works Brooklyn Festival at Brooklyn College. Directed by Elena Aaroz.

Your Healing is Killing Me premiered at JACK in Brooklyn, New York, October 5-7, 2017. Directed by Emily Mendelsohn.

Earlier drafts of parts of this manifesto have appeared in *Theatre and Cartographies of Power: Repositioning the Latina/o Americas*, *The Panza Monologues*, and the literary journal *The Thing Itself*.

This manuscript quotes directly from Sun Tzu's *The Art of War* and several online sources re: PTSD.

ACKNOWLEDGMENTS

To the artists who raised me with love and a whole lotta patience, including: Sharon Bridgforth, Laurie Carlos, Migdalia Cruz, Erik Ehn, Carl Hancock Rux, Omi Osun, and *raúlrsalinas*.

To the underground, the safe houses, the clandestine now named, comrades and comadres who have kept me fed and well taken care of, always, including: Maribel Alvarez and Patricia Espinosa-Artiles, Norma Cantú, Jennifer Cardenas, Monique Cortez, Karen Cellini and Joe Corcoran, Jackie Cuevas and Jen Margulies, Erica Edwards and Deborah Vargas, Jennifer Flores Sternad, Alan Gómez, Bárbara Renaud González, Alexandro Hernández Gutiérrez, Herminia Maldonado, Rafael Melendez, Dipankar Mukherjee and Meena Natarajan, Marissa Ramírez, María Salazar, and Kendra Ware.

To the ones who have helped build our Casa Chueca in the Bronx (so far away from Tejas), including: Blanka Amezkua, Netza Moreno, olaiya olayemi, Diana Perez Ramírez, Manny Rivera, and Rene Valdez.

To all the teachers and the professors who have taught my work and my writing over the years but especially to those whose invitations to their universities directly helped me articulate some of the ideas in this piece, including: Eddy Alvarez, Mary Pat Brady, Magda García, Tiffany López, Susan Mendez, Cristina Serna, Evelyn Serrano, and Helena Maria Viramontes.

To those who have read parts or all of this manuscript, including: Elena Araoz, Ricardo A. Bracho, and Nicole Fleetwood. With extreme gratitude to Emily Mendelsohn who was instrumental in the development of this script from page to stage.

To the team gathered by the good folks at Plays Inverse Press, including my super talented illustrator Zeke Peña and my publisher, Tyler Crumrine, who believed in this project.

To Maricella Infante, without whom nothing would get done, especially the laundry. I am immensely grateful for the everyday lessons you teach me about love and generosity and discipline, even when it kills you.

For the critical and thoughtful engagement of my ideas and my work.
For listening as I formulate the questions, the lists, and the 5-year plans I will later misplace.
For allowing me to dream.
For dreaming with me.

Gracias.
Thank you.

Introduction

"This is not a play," Virginia Grise tells us. It is a manifesto—that is, a program, proclamation, or pronouncement. Manifestos are often issued at climactic points in struggle as both a platform for action and as archive. In fact, the etymology of "manifesto" is a public declaration explaining past actions and announcing the motive for forthcoming ones. Grise's proclamation is an event/action that embodies the very disenfranchised bodies being killed off by neoliberalism. *Your Healing is Killing Me* is a manifesto for bodies in struggle, under attack, and the targets of structural violence. For Grise, our contemporary turn to healing as a primary response to the structural inequalities of white supremacy overlooks the ways "healing" has been reinvented through capitalist discourses of personal wellness. Discourses that, in turn, make us fit to tolerate structural violence rather than defeat it.

Grise urges us "to replace individual self-care with collective self-defense." Chairman Mao's 4 Minute Physical Fitness Plan—walk, reach, punch, present the bow, kick the door, side stretch, toe touch, to the heavens, jumping jacks, run—forms the organizational structure of this piece, and as we move through Grise's manifesto, our bodies are made fit to fight.[1]

Lately, I hear more and more people saying: "sitting is the new cancer" or "sitting is the new smoking" or to "stand up and move after 20 minutes of sitting." Correspondingly, Grise wants us to move. *Your Healing is Killing Me* is a movement manifesto—literally a call for us to move. People of color are masters of movement, having cultivated knowledges and grammars to survive forced displacements from their lands, homes, and kin. Our U.S. nation-state was built on systems of conquest and elimination: chattel slavery, wars and destructions of non-capitalist economies abroad, and the genocidal settler colonialism of First Nation peoples, among others.

"Collective self-defense" is not found in the personalized practices of healing, according to Grise's manifesto. In *Your Healing is Killing Me*, there is a distinction between self-care and safety, between persevering and healing, and between fighting and curing. Gloria Anzaldúa warned us long ago to be wary of the goals of healing from the destructions of structural racism, homophobia, classism, and sexism, drawing from her metaphoric description of the U.S.-Mexico borderlands as a geopolitical space produced from the grating of borders against each other and where the embedded-ness of poor/of color bodies are "open wounds" that constantly hemorrhage with no possibility of healing.[2]

For Grise, self-defense requires a self-care implemented in preparation to fight rather than to heal and tolerate. The healing Grise alludes to are those self-absorbed practices—those that result in our bodies feeling free of pain, trauma, and harm, and that can result in conciliatory tolerance of the social harms, environmental toxicities, and structural violence that Grise insists we name: dirty drinking water, gentrification, corporatized pharmaceuticals and health insurance. *Your Healing is Killing Me* calls on our bodies to be fit to fight.

Antibiotics are antibacterial, or a type of antimicrobial drugs used in the prevention or treatment of bacterial infections. We turn to antibiotics in the same accessible way our parents turned to aspirin. Generally understood, antibiotics heal us from an ailment by killing off parts of us (or killing the bacteria in our bodies). Antibiotics may or may not deter or inhibit the growth of the bad bacteria that harm us, but they can also kill off the good bacteria in our bodies—the good cells we need to fight illness, toxins, and disease. Capitalism acts like an antibiotic—its formula for healing, safety, and happiness requires the destruction and elimination of good: of solidarity with each other, with plants and animals, and with the earth. Grise's manifesto makes us pause to think about why we have become so desirous of healing rather than fighting what is killing us.

Your Healing is Killing Me is a manifesto that requires more from us than to simply heal ourselves—rather, it calls for transformation, transmutation, and transition of our bodies to be prepared for action. Grise's manifesto makes us cautious of the limits of healing because our bodies, minds, and spirits may become too comfortable, tolerant, and immune to capitalism's structural violence rather than capable of taking the action needed to defeat oppressive systems of power. Let us all move then with Virginia Grise—to kick the door, punch, move, and reach—as she summons our bodies to "Stand up! Fight back!"[3]

DEBORAH R. VARGAS is Associate Professor and Henry Rutgers Term Chair in Comparative Sexuality, Gender, and Race in the Department of Women's and Gender Studies at Rutgers University. Vargas is the author of *Dissonant Divas in Chicana Music: The Limits of La Onda* (University of Minnesota Press, 2012).

---

[1] Chairman Mao's 4 Minute Physical Fitness Plan was pressed to vinyl in 1973 by Celestial Arts, the very same year a three-month strike by grape laborers in Coachella Valley and San Joaquin Valley culminated in the shooting, beating, and arrests of thousands of workers. The record label states that Chairman Mao's 4 Minute Physical Fitness Plan includes "Authentic Music and Cadences Performed by the Central China Philharmonic Society," and one can occasionally find a rare copy on eBay or listen to the audio via YouTube.

[2] Gloria Anzaldúa. *Borderlands/La Frontera: La Nueva Mestiza*. San Francisco: Aunt Lute Books, 1987.

[3] One of the most popular chants by ACT UP (AIDS Coalition To Unleash Power) during the 1980s social movements was "What do we do? Stand up! Fight back!" Part of what ACT UP became known for was literally putting bodies on the line in social protest, with "die-ins" bringing attention to the number of deaths caused by AIDS and getting in the face of opposition in public spaces with loud chants and noise.

Your Healing is Killing Me is a manifesto, a meditation on political and artistic practice. When I taught theatre to high school and junior high school students in East Los Angeles, I started every session with Mao Tse-tung's 4 Minute Physical Fitness Plan. I cannot remember where I learned it from or who first introduced it to me, but 4 Minutes became a regular practice for my students. It was quick and precise and it taught discipline. For young people awkward and self-conscious about their own bodies, it taught them how to breathe together, to move together in unison as an ensemble, how to commit to actions that at first might seem quite utilitarian (walking, reaching, punching), but in order to maintain the integrity of our collective movement they had to set intention for and follow through on each exercise. They had to show up, be present in their own bodies, and stay connected to each other.

Your Healing is Killing Me utilizes Chairman Mao's 4 Minute Physical Fitness Plan as the basis for its gestural vocabulary. Illustrations throughout the text serve as a guide for performing the exercises. Do not skip over them. It only takes 4 minutes to cycle through the entire sequence.

Originally developed as a one-woman show, *Your Healing is Killing Me* can also be performed with three actors.

—V. Grise

CHAIRMAN MAO'S 4 MINUTE PHYSICAL FITNESS PLAN

Walking

1. Reaching
2. Punching
3. Present the Bow
4. Kick the Door
5. Side Stretch
6. Toe Touch
7. To the Heavens
8. Jumping Jacks

Running

YOUR
HEALING
IS
KILLING
ME

This is not a play.

I write plays set in bars without windows, lesbian bedrooms, and barrio rooftops.

I write plays about rape and sexual assault and dykes who enjoy fucking.

I write plays about queers that break down and fall out sometimes.

I write plays about state violence and mis-education.

I write plays about prison rebellions and armed revolution.

But this is not one of those plays.

This is a Manifesto.

Towards A Politic of Collective Self-Defense
Instead of Individualized Self-Care.

Exercise 1: Reaching

I am a working artist that lives in New York City. I first moved to New York with two suitcases, $300, and nowhere to go. I kept following the work from San Antonio to Austin, back to San Antonio, to Los Angeles, Minneapolis, Chicago, back to LA, now New York. My first spot in the city was a fifth-floor walk-up in the East Village. The bathtub was in the kitchen, under the cabinets, next to the sink. My friend Rafa let me sleep on his couch. At first, everything in a new city is an adventure, including getting lost. At first, at least.

I learned quick, you can't get on the train just because the door is open.
It might be taking you in the wrong direction!

New York is one of the most expensive cities in the nation. The average cost of rent is 50% higher than most cities in the United States. I pay $2,200 to live in a three-bedroom, fourth-floor walk-up in the Bronx.

A can of coffee costs $6.14.
A dozen eggs, $2.89.
In the winter, avocados are $2.79... EACH.

Growing up, my mother used to say:
Es que mija only rich people are artists.

They are the ones that can afford such leisure.
The implication being obvious:
YOU are not rich.

And my father repeatedly talks about how he disapproves of my lifestyle choice. "Lifestyle choice" to him does not mean sexuality. He doesn't seem to have a problem with that. In fact, he told me I was queer before I ever expressed my desire publicly for women. (I did mention I like dark bars without windows.) What he disapproves of is me being an artist. He can't even say the word:

Artist.

Instead he shakes his head and mumbles:

I don't understand.
Why would you choose that lifestyle?

Exercise 2: Punching

My father used to read the newspaper every morning before going to work. He is now 75, retired, and legally blind, but he still wakes up every morning at 6AM, makes his cup of coffee, and eats a bowl of oatmeal. Instead of reading the paper now he listens to the newspaper being read to him on a radio station for the blind. My father never graduated from high school. Recently, I found out that he never even went to high school, forced too young to choose work over school. Growing up it was a given that my sisters and I should read and think about the world around us critically and politically. My father believed that thinking critically and politically was everyone's responsibility regardless of one's education, race, class, or gender. He hated boredom and he hated ignorance. Still does.

When Ronald Reagan died, my father bought a cake. He went to the grocery store, bought a huge chocolate cake, and threw a party. My mother was horrified, thought it was sacrilegious, screamed and yelled and begged for forgiveness, "Ay dios mio, please stop it." He struck a match to light the candles and said, "Ronald Reagan was an awful man, Emma. He was an awful, awful man." He kept saying it again and again, "Ronald Reagan was an awful man. He was an awful, awful man," staring blankly at the wall in front of him. He lit all the candles of the birthday cake, blew them out, and then started to cry. It was one of the few times I remember my father crying growing up.

I think I was way too young to really understand what Reaganomics did to this country even though he did. The list was long: ignoring the AIDS crisis as the body count continued to rise, cuts to mental health funding, cuts to retirement benefits for veterans, cuts to social welfare for the working poor, cuts to Medicaid, cuts to financial aid for college students, cuts to taxes for the rich while simultaneously raising taxes on the middle class, attacking labor unions, and increasing government spending on the military.

As a kid, I spent most of my time in garages choreographing dance routines to Michael Jackson's "Thriller." I even had a silver sequined glove. Not a pair, just one. I'd wet my hair and put mousse in it pretending I had a Jheri curl. My mother tried to explain to me that Mexicans don't have Jheri curls.

> But what about Menudo, ma?
> They're Puerto Rican, she said.

A brown girl growing up in San Antonio, I had not yet learned that not all brown people were Mexican. And she apparently had not learned that Mexico was also part of the slave trade. At the time, I didn't really care to be honest.

You see, I just wanted to dance.

I started running away when I was very young, imagining the worlds beyond my neighborhood. I rode my bike to the cemetery, the railroad tracks, the ditch down the street, the corner store, the dirt road behind our house, up and down hills, around sharp corners. I learned about scraped knees, stolen flowers, and things girls at five shouldn't know, no matter how grown they think they are. And I made up stories set in far away places, like how I was born in a big blue house in California.

As a kid, I had an imaginary friend. Her name was Karla. With a K. She was a fast girl and a shit talker and, to this day, I like fast girls and shit talkers. Karla was the one who taught me how to say:

Motherfucker.

Or at least that's what I told my mom when she asked me where I learned that word. My father had read in one of his morning newspaper articles that creative, intelligent people have imaginary friends so he encouraged my mother to set a plate for Karla at the dinner table one evening.

My sister loves to tell this story. My mother made it halfway through dinner before she refused to continue playing my game of imaginary friend. She threw Karla's plate on the floor, breaking it, and then took me by the arm, kicking and screaming, to go see the curandera for some old skool healing.

This was one of many childhood visits to the curandera that involved flowers, huevos, smoke, a stranger spitting on me, and/or holy water. My mother was trying to cure me of my badness, but it only made me think that being Mexican was magic.

Exercise 3: Present the Bow

1.

2.

3.

4.

5.

Rose petal limpias
Marijuana leaves
Agua pura
Brown Chinese alcohol in a pickle jar

Rising smoke
Melting rock

The cold huevo on my forehead
Broken in a glass of water
Placed underneath my bed, yolk rising

When you wake up, breathe on it, before brushing your
teeth, un poquito de manteca de corojo y miel de abeja,
if you drop it on the floor you cannot touch it with your
hands, you have to pick it up with your mouth, drop it
in your palm.

I remember, or at least I think I remember, that one
night when, underneath a dark sky, my grandmother
took a white rock, held it in her hand, breathed on it.
Then she placed it on a black skillet and lit it with a
match. The rock melted. White rock, black skillet. My
grandmother and my mother and my two sisters were
all there. We performed this ritual behind the house
when my father was asleep.

Pa curar el susto, she said.
I must have been scared.

Some people get scared, so scared. Something has scared them so bad they leave their body. Some people die of fear even. The rock melted into whatever was causing the fear. Mine melted into the shape of a man and I had to jump over it three times. I was five. At age five I had already learned fear, had already learned to be scared, scared of men, scared of the men on the street in my neighborhood.

At age five,
I…
I…
I…

Exercise 4: Kick the Door

TEN CHARACTERISTICS OF PTSD

1. Recurrent and persistent recollections of the traumatic event, including dreams.

2. Acting or feeling as if the traumatic event is happening all over again.

3. Intense distress related to internal or external events that remind one of the traumatic occurrence.

4. Efforts to avoid thoughts, feelings, conversations, activities, places, or people associated with the trauma, including decreased interest or participation in certain activities, feelings of detachment, or estrangement from others.

5. The inability to have certain feelings.

6. A sense that time is short and there is no future.

7. Difficulty concentrating, falling and/or staying asleep.

8. Inability to control your anger or angry outbursts.

9. Hyper-vigilance.

10. An inability to remember important aspects of the traumatic event.

There are very few things I can remember about growing up, and the things that I do remember I am not sure if I actually remember those things or if it's that I've been told the story so many times that it's become a part of my memory. I used to think that your ability to remember started at age 12, that nobody actually remembered their childhood. I thought 12 was a rite of passage of sorts. It was the year I started menstruating, the year I started having consensual sex, the year I started to remember.

My father suffers from PTSD.
He did three tours of duty in Vietnam. When he went to war, my mother went back home to Mexico to raise my two sisters with the help of her mother. When my father returned from war, both my sisters only spoke Spanish. He only spoke English.

My mother suffers from PTSD.
When my mother was in Mexico, she received a letter telling her that my father had been killed in combat. It took her two weeks before she discovered that he was only injured. My father keeps his Purple Heart in a box hidden in a drawer. He never speaks about Vietnam. Instead, he took his silence out on my mother. My sister says that as a kid every time she heard the sound of an ambulance siren she thought my mother was dead, that my father had finally killed her.

My sisters suffer from PTSD.
I am eleven years younger than my oldest sister. She once told me that we had completely different fathers. The man he is today is just not the same man I knew as a child, she said.

I suffer from PTSD.

I am lost.

They say it's hard to do in New York because the city is laid out in a grid. Because it is laid out in a grid, they say it is the best city in the United States to live in if you are blind, which is good because, like my father, I am going blind. Streets run east to west, north to south, ascending and descending street numbers and avenues, uptown, downtown, midtown, not like San Antonio or Los Angeles, where streets sprawl out of control from the city's center. But I am lost. Again. And it's not like I have never been to the place I am going to—in fact I go there often—but today I cannot seem to find it. It's as if the city shifted in the middle of the night while I was sleeping. This happens to me quite often, things that were once familiar become foreign, things that are foreign never become familiar. And I am lost. Again. It doesn't matter that I have lived here for four years. I am always lost. I have even gotten lost going to my own home. I blame it on the subways. I feel like I lose my sense of direction traveling underground and I miss the sky. There is not enough sky in New York City. You'd think I'd be used to it by now, being lost, but instead it causes me great anxiety and a whole lotta fear because I know what happens to women when they get lost, when they are somewhere they shouldn't be, when they let on that they don't know where they are going...

Because No Space Is Safe.
This is a concept I learned at a very young age.

It sucks being a woman, huh?
Yeah, it does, I responded.

The nurse squats down next to me and holds my hand after I faint. I had lost too much blood and fainted. I didn't know I was pregnant, hadn't noticed the periods missed, didn't understand why I was getting nauseous or feeling faint all the time. I had even begun lactating.

Why did you wait so long?

I started getting my period when I was 12, the same year I started having consensual sex. I remember waking up, going to the bathroom in the middle of the night, and just screaming. I woke everyone up, crying and screaming, blood gushing. I was bleeding from the inside out and had no idea why. Why was this happening to me? I held on to the sink and I screamed. No one ever really explained what was happening. There are some things we just don't talk about I guess. My mother cleaned me up, showed me how to use a pad. Said wear this until it stops and that was it.

I felt like that 12-year-old girl all over again, not knowing how my body was changing or why. My roommate finally made me go to the doctor.

You're throwing up everything. You're losing too much weight, too fast.

I'm scared of doctors, of hospitals.

Do you want to see the ultrasound?

I didn't. I wanted it out. This thing, not yet born. Lodged inside of me. Making me sick. I wanted it out. I could have never talked to anyone in my family about my abortion. There are some things we just don't talk about I guess. I borrowed the money the first time. This was in February. By summer, I had had a second abortion. By January, a third. I always lie about it, when it comes up on medical forms or in conversations, even with best friends or lovers, men or women. The first abortion I will admit to without shame but I don't ever tell anyone I had three abortions in a little less than a year. I was 20.

The silence, not the abortions, created a great deal of trauma. Though I never wanted to have children, I started creating false narratives that equated being a woman with being a mother. It didn't help when, in my 30s, former female lovers started getting married, having children, and making families with other women and sometimes men.

I have never wanted to have children.
I have never wanted to be a mother.
I have never wanted to be a wife.

FOUR THINGS CIS MEN WILL NEVER HAVE TO DO

1. Menstruate.
2. Get pregnant.
3. Give birth.
4. Have an abortion.

Yeah, sometimes it sucks being a woman.

Exercise 5: Side Stretch

27 steps from my apartment to the front stoop.
2 flights of stairs.
5 steps down to the sidewalk.
7 blocks to the Nostrand stop.
2 flights down.
Take the A to Jay Street.
Transfer trains across the platform.
The F to Herald Square.
5 blocks to the Chinese Acupuncture School.
5th floor.

There is an elevator.
Most days it does not work.

My knee hurts. My qi is blocked. I am too hot inside.
An hour session used to be $20. Now it's 25.
A "DO NOT SPEAK CHINESE IN THE CLINIC"
sign hangs on the door.

I always ask my acupuncturist-in-training lots of questions. Today I ask, Why did you put the needles in my back? You don't normally do that. Eh, new moon, Eastern medicine, he scoffs. I'm not sure if my acupuncturist in training actually believes in acupuncture or Eastern medicine even. Maybe going to acupuncture school is something his parents made him do. I don't even know if I believe in acupuncture but I do like it when he sticks the needle in my forehead, right there between my eyes. Point #20 of 28.

For stress, he says.

I knock out cold every time. He turns out the lights. It's one of the few moments I sleep peacefully. One whole hour. Sometimes it's the most uninterrupted sleep I will get in weeks. He comes back to check on me:

Your job is very stressful, no?
Yes, I admit.

Do you like your job?
Yes, I have to admit.

Remember that the next time you sit down to write.

365 acupuncture points.
12 major meridian lines.

I go to the acupuncturist because I have eczema. On face value this doesn't seem like such a big deal, right? But my eczema is extreme. Allergies, rashes, hives, itchiness, dryness around my mouth and eyes, cracked and bleeding skin. Nobody can really tell you what exactly causes eczema but they think maybe it is a combination of factors that include: abnormal function of the immune system, genetics (which I continue to ignore), and environment.

Before I had health insurance as a working artist, before the Affordable Care Act, before I knew what I had was eczema, I had a black market doctor back in Texas. A physician who happened to be an incredible actor. That's how we met. She was in one of my plays. I would call her every time I had a flare-up. Send her pictures of me. Eyes swollen shut, that's how bad it was. I couldn't even open my eyes some days. My black market doctor in Texas would write me a prescription. Of what? I didn't even care but it would relieve the itching, the open, bleeding sores on my face, in between my fingers, in the folds of my arms. The creams were over $100 a tube and they were the only thing that would stop the itching. I later found out that the medication had steroids in it, so many steroids it felt like I was on testosterone. It was like I was transitioning and didn't even know it, but all of a sudden everything made sense: the rapid weight loss, over 50lbs, the mood swings and violent outbursts, including the time I banged on the hood of some man's car in the hood cuz I had the right of way god damnit.

I know you see me muthafucker.

I later found out that the medication with the steroids in it was also highly addictive. I quickly became dependent on it. If I stopped using it, my flare-ups would be even worse than before, so even though the directions on the tube clearly stated, "discontinue after two weeks if you do not see improvement," I just kept lathering the cream on my eyes, around my mouth, in the folds of my arms, and in between my fingers because the way I felt off the cream was far worse than the way I felt on it, until my black market doctor in Texas finally cut me off, saying that she was treating the flare-ups, the reaction, but not the cause.

I don't know what's wrong with you. You could have
an autoimmune disorder.
An autoimmune disorder?
Like lupus.
Lupus?
I think you need to see a doctor.

I think I've had eczema since my 20s but it always went
undetected or misdiagnosed. Even though my mother
also has eczema, far worse than mine, her response was
always, Your skin is too dry. You should use Pond's.
Mexican mothers think they can cure everything with
Pond's Cold Cream and/or Vicks VapoRub. So I would
excessively scoop Pond's Cold Cream out of the jar by
the handful until I found out that Pond's also flares up
my eczema.

While it is not an allergic reaction, certain factors,
including foods, can trigger eczema. Heat triggers my
eczema. I can't live in New York in the summer. Dirt
triggers my eczema. I can't take certain subway lines cuz
they are too dirty. And, of course, stress, stress triggers
my eczema. I am a working artist in the United States of
America. I have a lot of stress but I do like my job. I try
to remember that when I sit down to write.

I once did the Master Cleanse, for an entire month,
because a really cute hippie chick in Austin told me it
would help with my skin. She was fast and a shit talker.
So needless to say, I would do just about anything she
told me to do. This was before I was diagnosed with

eczema. You've heard of this right, the Master Cleanse? According to one website the Master Cleanse is "a liquid diet that provides a healthy amount of calories and nutrients specifically suited for weight loss and cleansing, all while resting the digestive system and allowing the body to heal naturally and has been tested and approved since 1940 by millions of people all around the world." Millions of people, all over the world, since 1940, said this was great. What could possibly go wrong?

So for an entire month I lived off of lemon juice, mixed with cayenne pepper and maple syrup. Flushed out my system with warm salt water before going to sleep and completely fucked up my digestive system. My digestive system was supposed to be resting! Now I can't eat foods high in acidity and citrus, including: lemon and lime; orange; grapefruit; papaya; mango; strawberries, raspberries, blueberries, all berries really; nightshades such as tomatoes and eggplant; most chiles, especially red chiles; chile japones; chile flakes; chile powder; paprika; and especially, of course, cayenne pepper. Essentially I can't eat most things Chinese and most things Mexican. All those foods trigger my eczema. I am the daughter of a Chinese Mexican immigrant. Do you see the irony?

I don't know what's wrong with you.
You could have an autoimmune disorder like lupus, she said.

So I started looking up lupus on the Internet. The worst

thing you can do when you are sick and do not know what is wrong with you is look things up on the Internet.

Hyper-vigilance.

A friend of mine intervened, pulling me out of the rabbit hole of health hysteria.

Why won't you just go see a doctor, girl?
I don't have health insurance.

That was far easier to say than admitting that I am actually scared of doctors, of hospitals.
And sometimes science even.

Go see my case worker. He'll see you for free. Free, honey. You just have to tell him you think you have AIDS.
Wait, what? AIDS?
Well, you don't know what's wrong with you.
Yeah but AIDS?
Smash the stigma, honey. The doctor said you might have an autoimmune disorder. AIDS is an immune disorder. The consultation is free and he's nice, really nice. Just go see my case worker.

So I take a train uptown to a free clinic in Harlem, wearing huge sunglasses to cover my swollen eyes and the open sores on my face.

Seated between a junkie and a hooker, the two women look at me and say:

What happened to you mami? You look awful.
You know it's bad when the junkies and the hookers
think you look awful.

What's wrong with you?
I don't know I respond and start to cry underneath my
huge sunglasses.
I don't know. I don't know what's wrong with me.
Nobody seems to.

After doing a full STD workup, the case worker, who
was really nice, takes me to his cubicle and says:
I don't know what's wrong with you.
But I'm going to get you in to see a doctor today.

He makes several phone calls. Tells whoever is on the
other end of the line:
You have to see her today.

Hangs up the phone. Click. And then the nice case
worker tries to help me apply for Medicaid. Apparently
my income was slightly above the level to qualify but
the nice case worker was determined to help me out.
He was going to find the loophole, the condition, the
possibility that would help me get insurance.

By Any Means Necessary.

He pulls out a long form and after too many questions,
he asks:

Do you have any mental illnesses?
No, I respond quickly.

Does anyone in your family have a history of mental illness?
No, I respond just as fast.

He asks the question again:
Does anyone in your family have a history of mental illness?
Uh, no, I say.

I'm going to ask you again, this time he says it slowly:
Does anyone in your family have any history of mental illness? Any-body. Anything. Depression, even. Depression is very common. Everybody gets depressed. Depression counts.

I feel like I am not answering the question the way I'm supposed to.
What's the right answer? I ask him.
I feel like I am answering this question all wrong.

I can't answer that, the nice case worker says. I can just ask the question one more time if you would like:
Do you or anyone in your family have a history of mental illness?
I said no.

Medicaid Denied.

I have never known how to play the system.

But the nice case worker did get me in to see a doctor that day. The doctor lady, who was also very nice, says to me: Normally I'd get in trouble for this but they are transferring me in two weeks so I'm going to run every test I possibly can on you.

I was tested for lupus, mercury poison, diabetes, high blood pressure, low blood pressure, cholesterol. I even got a pap smear which I hadn't done in over five years.

The next week I went back for the results and the nice doctor lady said: I told you. My boss wanted to know why I ran so many tests. I told him I didn't know what was wrong with you.
What's wrong with me? I ask.
According to the tests, nothing. But clearly there's something wrong with you. We can both see that.
So what do I do?
I don't know. Maybe you should see a dermatologist.

Another doctor? I thought on the subway train back home, defeated, sunk into my body, still wearing my big sunglasses to hide the open sores on my face, when a stranger comes up to me and says: You have eczema. It's pretty bad, huh? You itchy? My friend Julio on 42nd can get you some cream for that. You don't even need insurance. Just call him.

She hands me his number on the back of a sales receipt.

Julio on 42nd Street deals black market eczema cream. Did I even have eczema? Maybe I should just call Julio, but did I really want to get into another black market underground cream racket? Maybe I should just go see a dermatologist. This was out of hand already.

So I went to the best dermatologist in all of Manhattan, a fancy clinic in Soho that treats acne, administers Botox, and does face lifts for the rich. Eczema. The dermatologist said as soon as I walked in the door barely lifting her head from her clipboard.

Before I had even sat down:
You have eczema. It's extreme.

Then she prescribed me a cream. The whole visit was less than 15 minutes. Painless. Why am I so scared of doctors? Doctors are not scary.

Do you have health insurance?

But doctors operate inside a system that ultimately doesn't really care about your health. This cream is pretty expensive but it will do the trick. I went to the pharmacy right away, filled the prescription, opened the box, and found out the cream she prescribed was the same cream my black market doctor prescribed in Texas, the steroid cream. Yeah that one.

I shoulda just called Julio.

Eczema creams are killing me.

Prescriptions that address the symptoms but not the cause are killing me.

Health care that is not actually universal or free is killing me.

Processed food is killing me.

Oranges, carrots, and chile are killing me.

Monsanto is killing me.

My self-poisoning is killing me.

Rising rents are killing me.

Not being paid on time and checks that arrive late in the mail are killing me.

Reimbursement paperwork is killing me.

BPA, plastics, and toxic receipts are killing me.

White supremacy is killing me.

White liberals are killing me.

A two-party political system, where neither party represents my people, is killing me.

The lack of political imagination in this country is killing me.

Insomnia is killing me.

Any and all roles defined by prescribed notions of gender and/or family and domestic obligation, including doing the fucking dishes, are killing me. I blame gay marriage.

Being put on hold is killing me.

Moments of silence while I wait are killing me.

Fakers, biters, and careerists are killing me.

Pan-Latino(ism) is killing me, as Latino is not a politic nor an ideology and does nothing to prepare us to defend ourselves against what is actually killing us.

Exercise 6: Toe Touch

1... 2... 3... 4...

You need to learn to breathe, she said, the white feminist professor.

Let's practice now. In fact, everybody do this with me. Breathe in for 4 seconds. 1... 2... 3... 4... And out for 4 seconds. 1... 2... 3... 4...

Again.
Inhale.
Exhale.

A young Puerto Rican student from the back of the room yells, I can't breathe.

I talk to fairies, the other white feminist professor says. I build tiny houses for them in my backyard and talk to them when I feel a bit overwhelmed, when I feel like I can't breathe.

Sometimes I feel like I am going crazy, says the young Puerto Rican from the back of the room.

Don't use that language, the woman of color feminist professor quickly corrects her. I have to challenge your use of language, she says, finger waving in the air. We have to change the language used to talk about women. Language matters. As women, we internalize these daily microaggressions all around us every day. You are not crazy.

But right now that's how I feel, says the young Puerto Rican student.

I was invited to a university to talk about my work a month after the students at that university, mostly students of color, mostly women, mostly queer, all undergrads, took over the president's office for over 100 hours with a list of 21 demands to the administration addressing issues from lack of diversity to sexual assault on campus. After the sit-in was over, the student organizers were having a hard time keeping up with their studies, expressed issues of fatigue and anxiety, and, like the young Puerto Rican student, many said they felt crazy.

I get invited to talk about my work at a lot of universities but this was a unique experience. You could feel a sort of tension as soon as you walked onto campus, some may call it trauma, PTSD even. The Women's Studies Institute felt the urgent need to address this issue and quickly responded by organizing a brown bag luncheon on self-care because, as the other woman of color feminist professor reminded us, the black lesbian feminist writer Audre Lorde had once said (perhaps you've seen the meme on Facebook?):

> Caring for myself is not self-indulgence.
> It is self-preservation and that is an act of political warfare.

Audre Lorde died of cancer before she turned 60.

June Jordan died of cancer.

Sylvia Rivera died of cancer.

Ana Sisnett died of cancer.

Michele Serros died of cancer.

Laurie Carlos died of cancer.

Lorraine Hansberry died of cancer at age 34.

Octavia Butler died of a stroke. She had high blood pressure and suffered from depression.

Gloria Anzaldúa died of complications due to diabetes. It took them two days to find her dead body.

Is it crazy that I feel like this?
Is it crazy that I feel like I am going crazy? the young
Puerto Rican student asked.

Maybe you should take a walk in the woods alone, the
other white feminist professor said. Or a bath, a warm
bath. How about we break into five groups now: reiki,
fairy houses, intentional breathing, massages, nature
walks. Long before break-out groups were formed the
student who said that she felt crazy had left the room.

If we believe that self-preservation is an act of political
warfare, then we must not forget to ask the question:
Who are we at war with? Who are we fighting?

When those students forcibly stormed and took over
the president's office, they were clear who their enemy
was; they had a strategy, tactics, and a list of demands.

What do we want? JUSTICE!
When do we want it? NOW!

And in 4 days, 100 hours to be exact, the administration
agreed to meet every one of the demands made by the
students. In fact, if you go to their website today, the
21-point platform is listed on their site, and next to
each demand is a report on the administration's progress
meeting said demand.

Can you hear us now?
Can you hear us now?

Can you hear us now?

The students had been heard. So why did the young Puerto Rican student feel crazy? Why did the other students of color feel crazy? Why did the young queers feel crazy? Why did the young women still feel crazy? After the sit-in, they were expected to go back to class, to be good students again, to no longer disrupt the university, its mission, and its daily activities, but when the students were forced to go back to class, the university didn't seem very different to them at all. And it wasn't.

The project of the university—professionalization, the production of knowledge, the infrastructure, the means of production—has always been in service of the state. After the sit-in, that had not changed. The sit-in was an important victory, important reforms will be made because of it, but as the black lesbian feminist writer Audre Lorde also says:

> The master's tools will never dismantle the master's house.

The university is still not safe, the women's studies center inside of the university is still a part of that institution, and it is not safe.

No space is safe.

If we operate from the understanding that no space is safe we can begin developing the tools to defend ourselves from what puts us at harm. We can begin to acknowledge both the context and conditions in our communities that are causing us to suffer from mental and physical distress.

1… 2… 3… 4…
I count things when I'm scared…

5… 6… 7… 8…
It's a trick I came up with when I was little…

9… 10… 11… 12…
Gets my mind off what's bothering me…

13… 14… 15… 16…
Helps me with the ansia…

17… 18… 19… 20…
As an artist, I think my biggest fear is going crazy.

Exercise 7: To the Heavens

Lessons From Sun Tzu's 'The Art of War'

If you know your enemy and you know yourself,
you need not fear the results of a hundred battles.
If you know yourself but not the enemy,
for every victory gained you will also suffer a defeat.
If you know neither the enemy nor yourself,
you will succumb in every battle.

Strategy without tactics is the slowest route to victory.
Tactics without strategy is the noise before defeat.

When torrential water tosses boulders,
it is because of its momentum.
When the strike of a hawk breaks the body of its prey,
it is because of timing.

Some terrain is easily passable, in some you get hung
up, some makes for a standoff, some is narrow, some is
steep, some is wide open.
Appear where they cannot go, head to where they least
expect you.

Opportunities multiply as they are seized.

Swift as the wind.
Quiet as the forest.
Conquer like the fire.
Steady as the mountain.

Are you a Revolutionary?

1… 2… 3… 4…

Exercise 8: Jumping Jacks

Please set up a date and time for your Chicana friend from San Antonio, you, and I to meet and talk at my place. Directions attached:

From 42nd St. take the E train to 23rd St.-Ely Ave.
(one stop after 5 & Lexington)
Transfer at very front of train to the G,
Go two stops to Greenpoint Ave.,
Exit front of train.
Surface, look for big red church,
Go that way two blocks,
Right on Noble St.
Next block is Lorimer
My building is brick, big, red.
Ring 6F.
(Note: G train no longer goes to Queens Plaza as still depicted on subway maps.)

Bring 3 glass bottles of mineral water.
I reject all plastic.

I was summoned to the home of legendary composer and baritone saxophone player Fred Ho. Rene told me that Fred was strict—disciplined—about being on time. Do not be late or he will not see you. Plan to arrive 10 minutes early.

I was 5 minutes late.

Rang the buzzer 6F, finger trembling.
I run up the stairs, 6 flights.

There was an elevator. I did not see it.

Out of breath, I knock on the door.
It is slightly ajar.

From inside the apartment I hear someone say:

Come in.
I do.

Take off your shoes.
I do.

Turn off your phone.
I do.

Fred was lying on his futon. Candle lit on the end table.
Music playing on the record player. A stack of books by
his side.

I brought your water.
Put it in the fridge.
I do.

I was going to take you to eat pork buns but I'm too
weak to go outside. I had Rene order some though. They
are on the table. Serve yourself and come sit with us.
I do.

These books are for you, he says.

I had arrived here in the living room of Fred Ho because of a dream. I rarely remember my dreams so when I do, I pay extra attention. In this dream, I was at a cultural center, walking with men in suits who were introducing me to people, important people. We shook hands. Handshake, smile, move on, more important people to meet. Handshake, smile, move on. Until I was introduced to Chicano poet and revolutionary Raúl Salinas. Raúl, by matter of complete circumstance, was locked up in Leavenworth at the same time as the Puerto Rican nationalist Rafael Cancel Miranda.

Have you heard of him?
Cancel Miranda?

In 1954, in an attempt to raise visibility for the Puerto Rican Independence Movement, along with Lolita Lebrón, Andres Figueroa Cordero, and Irvin Flores Rodriguez, Miranda, armed with automatic weapons, launched an attack on Congress. Many Chicanos at Leavenworth, including Raúl, made friends with the Puerto Rican Independistas real quick and began organizing for better conditions in the prison from the inside through a prison-wide strike that landed them both in solitary confinement.

These interethnic and anticolonial formations in Leavenworth were linked to the larger prisoner rights and anti-prison movements across the nation but also to global rebellions all over the world. The prison rebellion was not just about reform. It was a collective act of self-defense as well as a pointing to something beyond the bars, an imagining of something, something better.

Once a street hustler, Raúl became an internationalist in prison. After being released, he opened a tiny bookstore in Austin, Texas called Resistencia. As a young artist and activist, Resistencia was my home. Raúl died in 2008. But there he was in my dreams.

You are late to the discipline action committee meeting, sister. Rene is waiting for you.

Rene ran the bookstore after Raúl died. After the dream, I called Austin right away. Lilia, who runs the store now, answered the phone.

Can I speak to Rene?
He's gone.
Gone?
Gone.

My heart started beating fast. I thought he had died.

He moved to New York.
New York?

This was even harder for me to imagine. What was a Chicano from El Chuco doing in New York City? Rene and I met up in a small Chinese restaurant in Midtown where he told me that he came to New York to study with Fred Ho and to organize a campaign to

free political prisoner Russell Maroon Shoatz. He la.
invited me to read at an event he organized. I read a.
excerpt from my play, *blu*. Fred was at that event. It was
the last time he would leave his house before he died.
I met Fred Ho when I was at a personal and political
crossroads in my life.

Do you like your job?
Yes, I have to admit.

Remember that the next time you sit down to write.

I had forgotten, gotten lost in the hustle. I know what
happens to women when they get lost, when they let
on that they do not know where they are going. Like
the young Puerto Rican student, I felt like I was going
crazy, trying to navigate a system without any tools for
self-defense because I was trying so damn hard just to
live in gratitude, for this work that I do like, for this life.

Just stop fighting, girl.

So I unclenched my fists but then I started having panic
attacks in the middle of the night. Trying to remember,
try to remember, try to remember to breathe.

1... 2... 3... 4...

Raúl came to me in my dreams. Raúl led me to Rene,
Rene led me to Fred.

...u are late to the discipline action committee meeting, ...ster. Rene is waiting for you.

Fred was dying. He had cancer.

Lying there on his futon in the living room he said:

I just have one question for you.
Are you a Revolutionary?
It is the only question that matters.

Fred Ho summoned me to his home because after hearing me read he wanted me to write about Russell Maroon Shoatz. From his deathbed, Fred was leading an organizing campaign to get Maroon out of solitary confinement.

Shoatz was given the name Maroon by fellow inmates. The word is used to describe Africans who escaped slavery in the Americas and formed independent autonomous settlements oftentimes together with indigenous peoples. Maroon earned his nom de guerre because he had escaped prison more times than any other man or woman in the history of the Pennsylvania Department of Corrections. When he began organizing with other lifers inside the prison, the DOC retaliated and put him in the hole. Maroon had been in solitary confinement for over 22 years CONSECUTIVELY, was 70 years old, and also quite ill. Fred was determined to get Maroon out of solitary confinement before either of them died. He wanted me to create an education campaign around stories of Russell Maroon Shoatz and what it means to be a Maroon, what it means to be free, for us to be free, in the 21st century.

The first poem I ever read publicly was in the juvenile detention center in Austin, Texas. Over 15 years later this has continued to have a lasting impact on my work: prisons, both literal and metaphorical, the boxes people try to put us in, and state violence are tropes that recur in my writing. Writing, in part, is my attempt to liberate myself from confinement, conventional rules, norms, and structures, an attempt to imagine freedom. I felt anything but free at that moment. I was an activist turned artist trying to find my way back to the organizing that shaped my early years of political development.

Promise me something, Fred said.
Promise me you will come back here and tell me these stories.

I will.

Within two months, Maroon had been freed from solitary confinement and released into general population. Two months after that Fred died. I went back to Fred's home and read him stories about Maroon until the day before he died.

i can see the mountains in the distance
if i could just make it to the mountains
disappear into the mountains
disappear into the night
away from here
over there
don't seem so far
so far away at all

that moment
that moment i laid blanket on barbed wire
and climbed over it
that moment i made it over the wall
i have never felt so free
i have never felt so free
in my entire life
i have never felt so free

i remember
the mountains
the night
the absence of light

try to hold on to that memory
in my dreams
try to hold on to that moment
try to hold on to memories
until they become feelings
sometimes i forget what it's like to feel
in here

but i remember
i remember what mud smells like, earth under feet,
the juniata river
but that night, that night i could feel
could feel my feet on mud, on earth
one arm to cover my face
right arm extended away

and i and i and i
ran

runmuthafuckarunmuthafuckarun
ran so fast fluorescent light bulbs exploded
runmuthafuckarunmuthafuckarun
ran so fast metal bars busted open
runmuthafuckarunmuthafuckarun
ran so fast the shackles on my hands and feet fell off
runmuthafuckarunmuthafuckarun
ran so fast i heard the breathing of runaway slaves
the sound of light bulbs exploding
metal bars busting open
the shackles on my hands and feet falling off
the breathing, their breathing, the breathing
the breathing, the breathing, the breathing of
runaway slaves

i run so fast i became a maroon

from here
over there
over there
don't seem so far away now
i am almost there
i am almost free
Run

RECIPE FOR BONE SOUP

2 pounds or more of beef bones (If you were to go to a grocery store about $25 worth but the butcher in the Bronx gives me the bones for free.)

1 onion

2 stalks of celery, cut into 2-inch pieces

2 carrots (I'm allergic so I leave those out.)

2 tablespoons apple cider vinegar

1 bunch of parsley

2 bay leaves

1 tablespoon or more of sea salt (I like the taste of pink Himalayan salt on my tongue.)

2 cloves of garlic

2 jalapeños (There is no need to take out the seeds.)

Preheat the oven to 450 degrees. Roast the bones and the vegetables together until deeply browned for 40 minutes, turning them once. Fill a large stockpot with 12 cups of water, add the salt and bay leaves. Scrape the roasted bones and vegetables into the pot along with any juices. Add more water to cover the bones if necessary.

Cover the pot. Bring it to a boil. Reduce heat to a low simmer and let it cook with the lid slightly ajar, skimming foam and excess fat occasionally, for at least 8 but up to 24 hours. The longer you cook it the better your stock will be.

My baby makes me bone soup on Sundays with jalapeños and a whole lotta garlic. Why does it taste so good? I ask. She says it's cuz she made it. I eat it every day now.

I quit the eczema creams and have since replaced them with bone soup. Apparently healthy skin begins in the panza, the gut, or at least in its lining. The amino acids and minerals in bone soup give us what we need for the continuous daily repair of the lining in our intestines. Bone soup builds immunity, helps with inflammation and digestion. Some say it even fights cancer. After all those visits to the nice lady doctor and the fancy dermatologist and the cynical acupuncturist, I found out that what I needed was right in my kitchen the whole time.

Roast the bones.
Open them up.
Scrape out the marrow.
My grandmother would suck the marrow out of
the bone.
Never waste any part of the animal while cooking.

An entire industry has been created around the idea of self-care without naming what is actually putting us at harm. Americans spend upwards of 7 billion dollars a year on gluten-free products but why aren't we asking the question what happened to our wheat? Our corn? Our rice?

Capitalism is toxic. No amount of body butter or eczema creams will act as a salve for its toxicity. As a system it cannot be fixed. The only way to defend ourselves against it is to destroy it. The only way to destroy it is to create something better. In the process, we must be willing to assess, to prepare, to study, to fight, but we must also be willing to listen to ourselves and each other, to change, to transform, to care for ourselves and each other.

It is a process.
A daily practice.
Embodied.

Do you like your job?
Yes, I have to admit.

I am an artist. And as an artist, I believe that my greatest creative project is to imagine something, something better, where our dreams matter, where as a people we are free.

Breathe.
Breathe with me.

1… 2…

1. Reaching

3. Present the Bow

5. Side Stretch

7. To the Heavens

2. Punching

4. Kick the Door

6. Toe Touch

8. Jumping Jacks

VIRGINIA GRISE is a recipient of the Whiting Writers' Award, the Yale Drama Award, and the Princess Grace Award in Theatre Directing. Her other published works include *blu* (Yale University Press), *The Panza Monologues*, co-written with Irma Mayorga (University of Texas Press), and an edited volume of Zapatista communiqués titled *Conversations with Don Durito* (Autonomedia Press). She earned her MFA from the California Institute of the Arts and currently lives at Casa Chueca in the Bronx.

Querida Vicki,

Your Healing is Killing Me asks questions, the Zapatista gift, a letter in response. Thank you for this, these questions, these *encuentros*, provocations and invocations, summonings, the certainty of knowing the need to know what is uncertain. Letters are always code, translation, and non-Catholic confessions. Well, this one is.

Four minutes. Thich Nhat Hahn just retranslated and reinterpreted 1500 years of Buddhist thinking, asking us to find *the other shore*, the being non-being of middle ways of other shores. Four minutes.

I think you had already left Austin. It was either 2000 or 2001. I'm resisting looking it up on the face-a-gram or inter-web. Campaign to end the death penalty had already been taken over by the ISO. There was probably about 3,000 people gathered to protest the continued support of the death penalty by then-governor, Bush Jr. (How do you not get into UT Law but get accepted to Yale?), and specifically the then-recent execution of Shaka Sankofa. At the University of Texas at Austin, students had spray painted *Amungme Hall* on the building named after Jim Bob Moffit, the profitman behind Freeport MacMoran, and later, in support of a strike (sick-out) by the UT staff, including the custodial staff, glued thousands of locks shut on the campus. Organizing against the annual police killings in East

Austin. Between Chiapas, Austin, and San Antonio we tried to circulate struggle. On this particular day, people gathered to circle the mansion, on the corner of Lavaca St. and 11th, on the southwest catty-corner from the state capitol.

Ok, maybe it was about 2k people, enough for the beginning of the march to meet the end and wrap around the mansion in symbolic containment… slogans, passion, organizing, people seeing their own power, multiplied across our genealogies. Across the street from the mansion, I remember there were a group of Buddhist monks, in orange, sitting. The orange attracted my attention. I kept walking. Every time I looped around to the entrance of the mansion and turned the corner right, in front of the capitol built through the convict-lease system, there they were across the street, sitting. What were they doing? What did sitting do? What did protest change? What is change? How can resistance sometimes support the structure, like an arc, as Esteva or Prakash might say? I saw them sitting and kept marching. I still see them sitting. I have questions. *Your Healing is Killing Me* helps answer them… with more questions.

Cataloguing and planning, conjunctural analysis, the aikido of saying, "Is that so." In this age of culpability, who builds the platform? Who stands on the stage? Whose imaginary is behind the doing, how can that imaginary be collective, convivial? What do agreements make possible? How do we unlearn vengeance? How do ve become soldiers in a war for care? What convivial tools do we retrofit to today, to condition the possibility of something else? How are these not new questions? How does the language of war open and limit?

The *rebel archive* (Lytle-Hernandez) of radical tenderness (Églantine on Volodine), rebel care, fierce tenderness, or fierce care, what do we learn in struggle? When my abuelo got pneumonia in Phoenix, that then progressed to multiple organ failures due to stereotyped mis-diagnosis and had to spend time at five different hospitals, there are so many specifics I can't name without breaking down—the corporate bottom line of profit, the 14th Amendment, corporate personhood reproduces itself on the backs of certain specific bodies... I'll leave it there. I learned to care for my *abuelo's* body, his skin, his joints, his muscles, his hair, teeth. That caring for his body was not what I was socialized (expected) to do? That was not my care-work, the *radical tenderness* necessary for men to care for each others' bodies. raúl used to say that at Leavenworth and Marion during the prison rebellion years in the late '60s and early '70s, and one can imagine now, you knew who your family was by the people who were next to you when the guards came in to knock heads, and who was there to care for your wounds after. That is what *raúlrsalinas* would say.

It's about a 40-minute drive to the women's prison in Arizona, depending on traffic on the I-10 and the hour. I've only checked the mileage on the inter-web, never wanting to actually look at the odometer. I don't like using the online access to the records of our friends inside. Sometimes we have to for different bits of information but they're our friends. Some people don't seem to understand that in the movement. These are our friends and family. They are not poster children for something bigger; unless they want to be.

Always remember, four minutes to prep to go inside: Dress code. Coded letters. Orientation to disorient. "Mute your hotness." Grow in love and understanding with folks… co-learning exchange. What is mutual? What is one-sided—and can't be any other way? What is care? What has it not been? How does care create community? What do we do on the outside to see there is no outside from the outside?

I read books in cycles that often times parallel, refract, weave together. *YHiKM* was read multiple times, and next to Adrienne Maree Brown, Antoine Volodine, the most recent Zapatista communiqués, Helena Viramontes, Isabel Allende, and Juan Carlos Villalobos, the assigned readings in a graduate seminar on social transformation, and HBW readings. Particularly *Emergent Strategies*, which brought back the discussion sparked by an article written by B. Loewe, "An End to Self Care," and Brown's response at the time too, kept coming up, sorta like the monks sitting at the march. Each time I returned to *YHiKM* there were more questions that I could only ask in a letter.

Can the militant see the art in the insurgency? Can

there be an insurgency without militant art? If pronouns seduce the subjunctive then who is the subject of revolution? Perhaps a machete is the appropriate algorithm for kaleidoscoping negatives? How can tying knots free the negative from its own echo chamber? What plants grow in the mirror's shadow of yesterday? Can they poison fascists with "the smell of bitter almonds" (García Márquez)? Can we imagine how freedom pierces incarceration with multiple authors? Or is that kind of love reserved for dizzy acrobatic pronouns? Why are mid-sentence time-zone atmospheric earthquakes so delightful? If the war on grammar is grammatical then who sings lullabies to the sloth? Who do pronouns betray when they escape with adverbs? Who fears the unnamed author, renamed in polyamorous pronouns? How can art get people out, not of their heads but the walls? How can we organize affect?

If we scale creative resistance, undercommons and railroads, maroon trajectories, *lines of flight looking for a weapon* (George Jackson), then someone has to make sure we go to the mountain pass to see the sunset, to meditate on "How do you undo vengeance?" To sit across from the march, to see how scaled creative resistance and maroon communities are the same as going to the mountain pass to see the sunset, the same as holding someone tight after heartbreak, the same as finding refuge for the abandoned, the same as breathing: four minutes to the other shore.

I want to share with you in this letter how you saved my

life, how the Z's saved ours, how we save each other's and others', and others save ours, how the questions about politics, art, everyday relations, the questions about dignity and who is limiting our dignity, and choices about art, cultural work, knowledge production, creative thriving precisely because surviving is killing us. I know my healing has killed others, that my contradictions create coercive consent. You say, "It's hard watching my brother fall apart." Men fall apart. Men fall. Apart. Alone. And that kills others. How can we be healing's self-defense army of dreamers, and work our way out of the labor of war?

I travelled with Fred, raúl, and Magdalena once, during their West Coast tour (San Pancho, Cruz, Sacra and Bezerkeley) of jazz poetry. Fred was about timing (don't be late for the meeting, four minutes, breathe, breathe) and raúl was too, but on a different register. At the New School, before it closed, in front of part of the Third World Left left in the bay, in the heart of gentrifying *La Mision*, there was a moment where Fred was waiting for raúl to find the appropriate poem, and raúl was shuffling through his papers, turtle-pace, and you could feel the momentum building the moment, the quiet in the auditorium, the four minutes. raúl found the poem, Fred freed the notes, Magdalena brought the word. It's always about timing, and weaving those calendars.

Surviving is killing us and we die to survive. How do we theorize justice in the everyday? The Zapatistas ask us to create *semilleros*, seedbeds. What seeds will you save?

What do you see, sentinel? Who do you walk with? We have been walking together for decades, with others, Acción Zapatista, the *fierce care ateneos* of Unitierra-Califas, and the other unnamed collectives. How has art saved the imaginary from itself? How can we use our convivial tools: agreements, encuentro, coyunturas, to lead by obeying? How can radical care and tenderness already contain the possibility of self-defense? How is self-defense also about defending the/our bodies of people targeted for killing? Who has the right to self-defense? Whose geography and calendar marks and locates our healing? How is humor both balm and fire? How do we resist colonization by the alphabet? How do we destroy the language of development... not use it, when, for example, creative place-making is simply the artistic development of gentrification? What does it mean to create art in a time of war? What does it mean to use and move beyond the language of war?

"The truth is, the world don't want us. It never did," he'd say. But what world? Where? What would Jiko do? How do you let go of the need to heal?

YHiKM is about agreements. All spaces/relations have agreements, but not all are made transparent, and not all agreements are agreed upon, where coercion and consent seduce clarity. What do we do when we are scared? Flight-fight-freeze-fawn (thank you, Lola). What if we shared these things, talked about them, next to each other in these moments? Rather than judge, compare, make a scale, a hierarchy of humanity, call-out culture becomes fall-out culture without self-reflection, humility, admitting mistakes, not punishing each other like the state.

YHiKM is the Zapatista "One no, many yeses," where we all can name how we die because of someone else's life, how we live because others die, where the accounting dizzies.

I know the yous in this script; I learned about you in this script. I learned about me in this script. How that absence of remembering is a memory that remembers for us, another life, other lives, other pasts, paths, futures, memories live right next to us, walking with us, poking at us, supporting, sometimes rightfully angry. You already know much of the rest, the contradictions, invoking the surface moments of public and private violations.

I have been leaky. Leaking loyalty, leaking jealousies. Leaking uncertainty, fear, small vomits of healing turmeric. Leaking futures and poems, late in the day, in the hours after time changes and shadows feign sleep. The counting is a silly face, leaking poem, lost, found, rehomed, claimed, denied, how much is denial valued? "I'm in love with someone who doesn't know my family. What does that mean? Whose family I don't know."

Leaking responsibilities.
Litter-ness, holding hands,
Leaking solidarities.

Leaking thoughts, open categories.
Leaking care yet to happen.
Somewhere in the leaky glances,
Electric beadwork, summers, alternative time zones,
I want to ask her: Why did you never send me a package
to heal me, don't you have knowledge…
To help us heal, breathe, live my story as yours too, if
you asked?

Leaking to fill space. Emptyingness. But those memories
are far away—again. A creature of habit, and when the
habits are bad, a habitual creature. Every day a river
runs, somewhere, naked through sand, bits of Earth's
flaked memory, smooth wounds, healing the killing.
Accepting the invitation to do the dance of death when
everyone laughs at your rhythm, suspects your beat,
denies that there is even a dance.

YHiKM is subjunctivating: what if, what will, I hope it
does, I wish it hadn't, if only, if only, we dream, lament,
regret, hope, plan, revolt, seduce, and anticipate in
the subjunctive, not the future, not the past, but there
are past and future subjunctives. What if, would have,
would be, could be, the subjunctive different from
the future tense that is so sure in itself, the I wills, I
will not, because there is no future promise, other
than tomorrow coming, but tomorrow is not a future
without the subjunctive made real in struggle, without
imposing a future, we gather to sit and ask questions,
again. That's where the Zapatistas and the Buddhists
come together for me.

Not everyone knows how to write letters anymore or receive them for that matter. I've written letters, handwritten and typed to my mom and abuelo's friends and family on both sides of the walls, across borders, family in the sense of making our loved ones ours through care and kindness, sometimes tricking calendar and geography, for going on 20 years. Cuz it's a different mind, writing a letter, mailing it across a time zone, border checkpoint, surveilling guard, or zip code, the story therein, the feeling and wishes, fears and uncertainties, the questions for consummation and feeling wanted and cared for, are out there, waiting for an internal ear, waiting for response. Life goes on as that letter reaches another place, on the other side of wall, a fence, a street that marks safe from not, never safe, for whom and why?

What if through theater we could fly across these walls and borders, and not just like *voladores*, but exactly like voladores *on the inside* spinning on chairs, unthreading the orange, laughter shaking the bars. And that's the thing about this question about humanities and art and abolition and getting people out: Regardless of the answers, the "how" of constructing underground railroads, undercommons, community structures of fierce convivial care, *radical tenderness*, we have to engage on all fronts, as the culture of punishment and cruelty is a deep sickness of USian democracy, a settler colonial virus, it's economic and psychological, it's aesthetic and academic, it's political and social, it's the paradigm. Abolition is the only artistic question ever worth asking? I know that sentence is not syntactically correct. But you get it.

YHiKM is a seedbed: Zeke's art, Deb's intro, the color, the stories, the struggle to write through this struggle to write, itching words that don't go away when scratched, seeds planted below and to the left, sustained by the light of an *underground periscope*. We have to think simply, epically, like an organized landslide, otters holding hands in sleep, against the current like the salmon. We know no other way. We have to listen closely to those who speak in a language other than words, with subjunctive meanings, meanings with alternate interpretations, *lines of escape* interpretations with multiple possibilities, possibilities with fierce care, fierce care with careful practice, fierce care in ourselves with others, fierce care as self-defense, self-determined care as Brown invites.

We committed to raúl's and Fred's memory to continue the struggle for freedom for people in prison, political prisoners, young people targeted by the state—police, teachers, neighbors as patrollers, for our own freedom from and for ourselves, from patriarchy, the trappings of classism, the genocidal judgement about who we love, the unlearning of loving the intimate enemy.

YHiKM is historical reckoning: settler colonialism conditions spaces of unfreedom: the reservation, the prison, the gentrified barrio. Mexico was part of the slave trade. We are all walking contradictions. The

cream, pain, Karla, all markets are informal. You like your job. That's amazing. Cuz it's not a job. Work is not labor. Sometimes we don't know what is wrong, that something is even wrong. How do we go beyond solidarity, beyond survival and self-care, not as a hierarchy, but a political question? How is abolition revolutionary?

Let's learn to be otters: holding hands when we sleep so we don't float away in the river. See you soon.

A tired sentinel,

Alan Eladio Gómez
August 2017
Coyoacan, D.F.

PD: Long live the subjunctive!

ALAN ELADIO GÓMEZ works at ASU, lives and writes in the greater Phoenix metropolitan area, and is the author of *The Revolutionary Imaginations of Greater Mexico: Chicana/o Radicalism, Solidarity Politics & Latin American Social Movements* (University of Texas Press, 2016).

Since 2015, together with my partner Maricella Infante, we have intentionally been building an artist ecosystem inside our home in the Bronx. We have turned our living room into a salon, a rehearsal space, a theater, a convening site, and (on some nights) a cantina. Our spare room has been an artist residency, an emergency shelter, temporary housing, and (on some nights) just a place to crash when you are too tired to go home. And, over the past two years, we have fed a whole lotta people from our tiny kitchen. Casa Chueca is the heart of my artistic practice: intimate gatherings, active systems of support and care, knowledge and skill sharing, collaborative acts, and collective dreaming. We call our home Casa Chueca cuz ain't nothing straight in our house.

ARTIST SALONS AT CASA CHUECA (2015-17)

Blanka Amezkua
Rafa Esparza
Silvia Federici
Laurie Ann Guerrero
Kristiana Rae Colón
Mai'a Williams

We also currently host the Sobremesa Series, a monthly gathering of artists, activists, and intellectuals of color.

—V. Grise

Artists who have stayed at Casa Chueca (2015-17)

¡Aparato!
Hilario Alonso
Ben Barson
Moises Baqueiro
Adam R. Burnett
Chela Chelinski
Russell Craig
Drew Garces
Fernanda Garcia
Gizelxanath
Alexandro Hernández Gutiérrez
Laurie Ann Guerrero
Danny Herrera
Maria Maea
Christine Marie
Emily Mendelsohn
Rafael Melendez
Nancy Mendez
Netza Moreno
Andrea Negrete
Lisa Nevada
Miguel Pasillas
Kristiana Rae Colón
Manny Rivera
olaiya olayemi
Omi Osun
Ni'Ja Whitson
Raheleh Minoosh Zomorodinia